A World of Wonder

Olive H. Forgatsch

This, the first edition of this book has been limited to one thousand copies.

This is book number 339.

Printed by: News Printing Company
Goshen, Indiana

A WORLD OF WONDER

Poetry for Children

Written and Illustrated by
Olive H. Forgatsch

Rainbow Children's Books, Inc.
P.O. Box 513
Goshen, Indiana 46526

LIBRARY OF CONGRESS
CATALOG CARD NO.: 82-90106
ISBN Hard
0-9608784-0-8

Rainbow Children's Books, Inc.
P.O. Box 513   Goshen, IN 46526

Dedicated to:
All children everywhere who wonder

Wonder and awe about created things is the beginning of awe and worship of the Creator.

Acknowledgements

The enthusiasm and interest of my fellow teachers and administrators at Syracuse Elementary School first planted the thought that these poetry posters should be published. I am indebted to them for their encouragement.

My family was interested, helpful and patient. Friends were excited and encouraging. All those who in any way were of assistance share my deepest gratitude.

Lois Schoeff typed the first manuscripts.

John Naab had confidence in the project.

Nicholas Lindsay, poet-in-residence at Goshen College, read the manuscript.

Dorothy Hamilton encouraged the work.

To all of these, and all others who in any way had a part in the publication of the book, I am forever grateful.

Table of Contents

A World of Wonder

A world of wonder waits for me.
　　It's there within each growing tree,
It's hiding in a splashing brook,
　　Inside the covers of a book.
I see it smile in eyes of friends,
　　And in the stars when daylight ends,
But I must set my thinking free
　　To find where wonders wait for me.

Winter's Prank

The March Wind came
with shouts and a roar
That shook all the windows
and rattled the door.
He bowed grass and bushes
and tree-heads down low.
"I'll blow away Winter.
He'll soon have to go."

He blew and blew
          and   Winter   ran   fast,
But   laughed   as   he   hurried,
          "Just   one   last   big   blast.
I'll   cover   the   whole   land
          with   huge   heaps   of   snow,
And   then,   oh   yes,   then
          I   will   just   have   to   **go**,

And let fair Spring
       come dancing along
With leaf-buds and flowers
       all singing a song."
"I came like a lion
       with shouts and a roar.
I'll leave like a lamb
       and just slip out the door."

Amaryllis

But I know . . .
    If I cut it all apart
    I'd never find
         the reason
The amaryllis
         at our house
Has gorgeous blossoms
In its season.

Hilltop Thoughts

High on a hilltop
    I stood looking down,
And there, far below me,
    I saw the whole town.
Oh, how like a giant
    I watched toy cars go,
And match-stick-sized people
    that ran to and fro.

How big I am.

Resting my hand on
   a near by old pine,
Whose **body was** ten times
   as far 'round as mine,
I looked where its top reached
   way up in the sky
And sighed as I whispered
   to winds floating by

      Ah, no.
How small am I.

The strong wind MARCHED across the hill
And whistled a cold, loud song.

He brought a breath
of winter chill,
And carried the grass
and dried-out leaves
along.

He gives the month its name.
It's MARCH.
And he can bring
lion-like storm

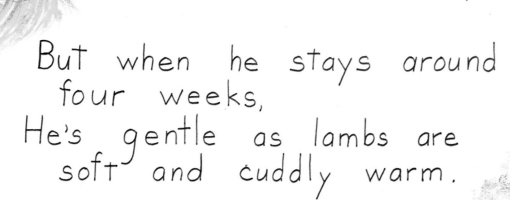

But when he stays around
four weeks,
He's gentle as lambs are
soft and cuddly warm.

So in like a lion,
and lamb-like out,
From howling, cold
winds to song.
A promise of April
in a shout
Of joy,
        that spring
is a gift he brought along.

18

Leprechaun Gold

A leprechaun, the Irish say,
Has hid a pot of gold,
And if you catch him, hold him fast,
He'll say just where, I'm told.

I caught this one and held him bound.

It turned him hard as stone.
No word he said, no gold I found.
Deep sadness I must own.

His elfen face I often searched.
At last the truth I hold.
How could we all be so confused?

His smile's worth more than gold.

Snowdrops

While everything else
Was frozen hard,
It grew.

Where ever the snow
Melts down a bit,
It pokes
Its head right through.

Egg Shells

When you crack an egg, the Irish say,
Be sure to crush the shell,
For there countless fairy folk
Still living in the dell,

And they could use an egg shell whole
Just like a fairy boat.
Away beyond the island shores
The tiny boats could float.

They want the fairy folk to stay
To bring good luck and charm.
So have a care, they'll get away.
You'll have bad luck and harm.

Seasons

Like the ocean's endless tide,
The seasons come and go,
And spring will surely come again
To follow winter's ice and snow.

IT'S SPRING

The sun comes out
    To melt the snow.
It warms the earth
    So iris grow.

The birds come back.
    They chirp and sing.
Butterflies flit.
    We know it's spring.

26

Spring's Birthday

Spring's Birthday came on tiptoe
The twenty-first of March.
The sun rose with a golden glow
To light the sky's blue arch.

The gifts that Birthday brought us
Were blooms of every kind,
Some windy days and sunny days,
And some trailed clouds behind.

Some other gifts were new grass,
Warm showers, dew and bees,
The lake as smooth as mirror-glass,
A honeysuckeled breeze.

MARSHMALLOW BUNNY

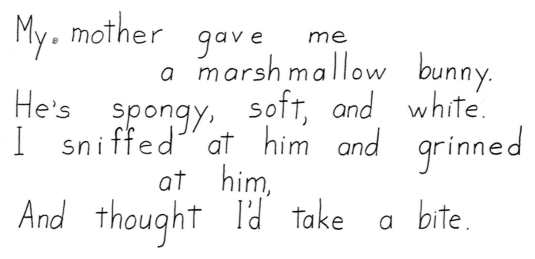

My mother gave me
        a marshmallow bunny.
He's spongy, soft, and white.
I sniffed at him and grinned
        at him,
And thought I'd take a bite.

I first bit off one long, thin ear,
And then a foot I tried.
But when I ate that puffy tail
I'm sure that bunny cried.

Spring Fever

There's a robin in that
tall oak tree.
He's hopped to the
highest branch
I see.

	Math	
81	204	7
5	115	9
68	714	6
21	342	5
563	402	5
114	163	9

Just can't get this math into my head.

"Be sure to add <u>ones</u> first," the teacher said,
"Now the <u>tens</u>, then hundreds last."

Wait. I got lost!
Don't go so fast!

What happened
        to that
              robin
                  now?

Oh, there he is
      on a lower
            bough!

Ugh, math. How did that
go again?
Ones, hundreds, and then
the ten?

$$467$$
$$-32/$$

He's gone.

6
7

$$532$$
$$-121$$

$$146$$
$$201$$

No, back with a worm
he flew.

15
2

$$562$$
$$124$$

M-m-m--math. Six plus two.

4
3

Oh look, I think he's going to sing.

Well, let's see. I can't do that thing.

I think I did that problem wrong.
At least I heard the robin's song.

April Is a Girl

April's tears are flowers
and new green shoots
of corn.
April's smiles are sunbeams,
pink-gold in springtime
morn.
April's curls are cloud-puffs
spread 'round a sky
of blue.
April's a girl most lovely,
a breeze caressing you.

FLYING

Superman needs a cape
A kite flys on a breeze
An engine makes an
    airplane go,
But I just need
    some skiis.

I skim across the
    wave,
Make the spray fan
high.

I jump the wake, then back again.
My water skiis make me fly.

Sparkling creek in the quiet wilderness
Tumbled over boulders and sang a gurgling song,
Washed the pine tree's feet and went hurrying along.
Pine tree stood with the mountain at its back,
Stretching to the blue sky, and sighed the gurgle song
Back to crystal stream and the silence of the sun.

TEETH

Most all my friends had lost a tooth,
Or two — or maybe three.
I still had all my baby teeth.
Was something wrong with me?

I wiggled them and twisted them,
I tried so hard to find
Just one of them a little loose.
I almost lost my mind.

And then I lost them — one, two, three,
Four teeth right in a row.
The bottom ones just popped right in.
Now see those new teeth grow.

I wonder now what's wrong with me
That top teeth still are gone.
I looked,
        and hoped,
                and sometimes cried.
No front teeth,
            not one,
                    not one.

And then one day a tiny point
Pushed through the pink to show.
Now I will have my two front teeth,
Now I'm OK
            I know,
                I know.

RAINBOW

I saw a rainbow arched up round.
Its center reached where birds can fly.
The ends came down to kiss the ground
While tears dropped from the darkened sky.

I saw it really was quite near.
The woods were

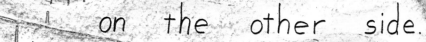

on the other side.
One end, you'll be surprised to hear,
Was right here on the meadow wide.

But then I tried to walk to it.

It moved.
        I know it really did.
When I got there,
            'twas gone,
                    thats it

Around
        behind
                the
                    hill
                        it hid.

I hoped that I could catch and keep
The colors bright, the bow up high.
No, leave it for the rain to weep,
Then pull the bow back to the sky.

Just let it come to us again.
I want to see its colors bright.
I'll wait for sunshine mixed with rain
And wish for it with all my might.

Ocean's Tricks

Purple starfish on wet sand,
Seaweed tossed up on the land,
Waves smashed hard upon the shore,
Sand washed out to sea once more,
Constantly, and day by day,
Tricks the ocean likes to play.

Rain

Did you pause to watch the rain
A-splashing on the window pane?
It makes a path down from the top
   That grows and grows, drop by drop.

I look from my soft warm chair
   And see the rainbits breaking there,
   And hear the thunder-drums loud boom
That rattles doors, shakes the room.

Rain that keeps me safe inside
Will sprinkle flowers far and wide,
Until the hillside's bright and gay,
As rainbows spilled, dance and play.

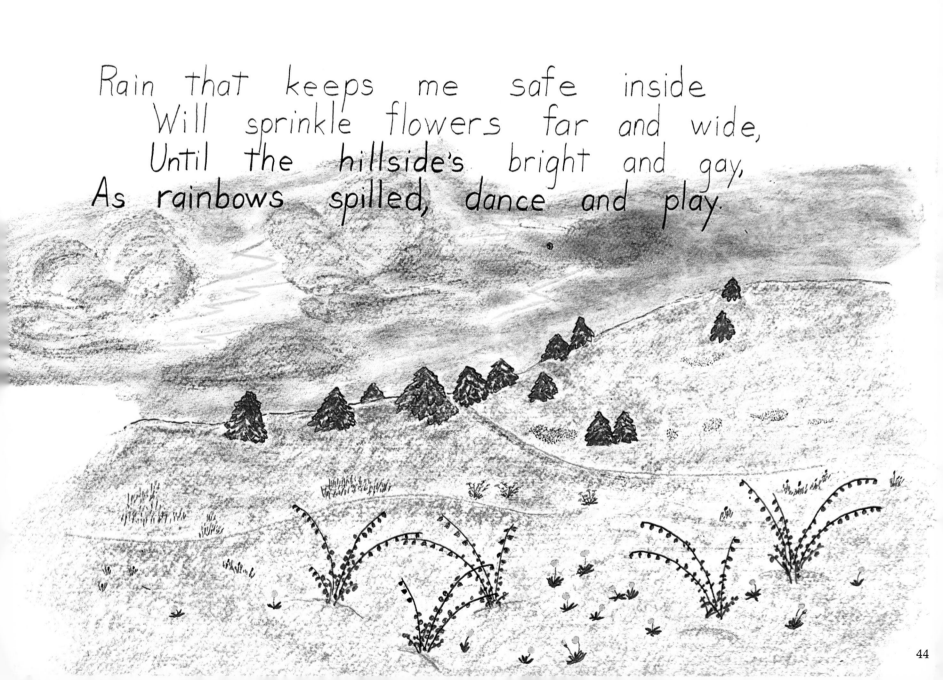

JETS

I wonder where that jet will fly
On its long flight across the sky.

How far away and to which town
Will this jet go, and where come down?

It leaves a trail fanned out pure white.
Sun turns planes silver with its light.

I wonder if a boy rides it
Excited — happy — scared a bit —

Each time I see a jet go by, I wonder,
wishing I could fly.

46

Music of Spring

The daffodil lifted its golden head.
"The springtime has come—
                    it's already here."
It looked all around then
                    whispering said
"The happiness time,
                    the best of the year."

The daffodil whispering
made a spring song.

The raindrops came tumbling
                down from a cloud.
A drum-beat for rhythm
                they made on the walk.
"It's time to awake," they beat it out loud.
"It's time to awake. Come
                leaf-bud and stalk."

The drummer kept time
for the daffodil's song.

The leaf-buds and grasses were
                first to rise up,
But others stirred sharply
                and harked to the song
The tulip came softly
                then each buttercup,
And joined in the chorus
                the bluebells rang long.

A melody rings in the
chorus they sing.

The spring smell of washed earth,
                    a new flower bed,
Of green grass and ponds
                    and new leaves on trees,
All blended with perfume of
                    each flowering head,
Hung lightly, then floated
                    along on the breeze.

So perfume and rhythm
identify spring.

The flavor of spring is
                    a strawberry   sweet,
And   creamy-green   stalks
                    of asparagus   new,
The   sparkling tart of
                    a rhubarb pie treat.
It's crisp curly lettuce and
                    radishes,   too.

Flavor and crispness
add accent to rhyme.

Yet color's the center
of springtime sweet thrill.
Eyes drink up the brightness,
a rainbow, a cloud,
All senses awake from
dull winter's damp chill,
Rejoicing together, spring
singing aloud.

All join in a symphony,
joyful springtime

JUNE

June is a laughing, lounging, lazy time,
    Lying in the sun,
Planning days of no school work,
    Days of naught but fun.

June is for swimming, fishing, skiing too,
    Playing on the beach,
Building castles in the sand,
    Just outside waves' reach.

June is a dreaming, listening, thinking time,
    School won't bother me.
Clouds make monsters, bees still hum,
    Wonders rare to see.

Learning without a schoolbell, book, or pen,
    Really can be fun.
Summers' Nature teaches me.
    Autumn comes, it's done.

I'd never trade the school for summer days,
    Summer days for school.
I need both to grow, you know,
    That's life's growing rule.

OLD OAK TREE

They're building houses
on our street
And that is just
as it should be.
There is one place not for a house.
Just that one spot is for a tree.

An old gnarled oak has stood right there
Three hundred years, its branches high,
And when they cut that old oak tree
I know its fall will make me cry.

Wonders

If I explore the whole world wide
The sky, the earth,
the ocean tide,
I never still could really see
Where all the wonders
wait for me.

Note to readers:

The poetry posters for this book were developed over the past ten years to be used in the classroom. Children enjoyed them and were enriched by growing with them.

To be able to touch a child's life and expand his understanding is a precious gift. The poetry stretches the imagination and inspires awe and wonder about the world of nature around us. It explores fantasy and legend. It fosters a love for beauty of expression.

To share this gift, not limiting it to a classroom, became my desire. So, this book in the hands of a child will open doors of wonder and build enduring values.